GRAVEL ROADS

and other journeys

To Mom & Dad
The family fire
is all we have
to huddle around
when the wolves
come...

love
MRP

sept
2013

Michael Ray Perkins

Published by Cider Press Books
Copyright © 2013 Michael Ray Perkins
All rights reserved

Edited by Jessica Walsh

ISBN-13:
978-1490972800
ISBN-10:
1490972803

www.michaelrayperkins.com

II

Dedication

For all my family — thank you for everything. And for Kathy Yount and Alan Charbonneau, my only teachers in high school.

Preface

We all begin somewhere, and as it happens, I began on a gravel road in the heart of Missouri. I didn't stay on those roads but traveled to other places on many journeys. Yet as I think about it, I never left those country lanes, and they certainly never left me, even though they're paved over and barely recognizable. Time has put a veneer over both of us that hides our true origins from the casual observer.

But poetry is more than a casual observer and can transcend the boundaries of time. The gravel roads are still there. I'm still here. But we no longer have the '57 Chevy. We do, however, have our memories ... and our poems.

Table of Contents

Gravel Roads

they lead home
rather than
pass by anonymously
no exits, just
driveway and gate entries

winding descendants
of animal trails,
Indian highways,
cattle paths,
and farm lanes
organically following
the spine of the dragon
naturally balanced
aligned according to
the tenets of feng shui

A Convertible at Night

relief from a corrosive sun
nothing like it
in the summer

driving with the top down
on cursive roads
full of turns

night bugs splatter the glass
a contemporaneous chorus
of cicada sacrifices

Cowgirls

the young ones want
something a little wild,
a little mean, and fast
something to ride rough
bareback for pleasure

the old ones, something gentled
broke to the saddle
not likely to misbehave
drop the reins
and they wander back to the barn
on their own

cowboys are just about the opposite

The Party

walking into the room
the buzz takes you
nothing but brain static
white noise

surrounded by dramatic vignettes
strolling through one production
after another
like channel surfing
sitcoms, dramas, and love stories

overhearing tidbits
drifting in the air
pieces of conversation
mirthless canned laughter

emotional groping and groveling
something in the air is sticky
essence of estrogen and testosterone
makes you feel unclean

nobody even knew you were there
after you leave incognito
nothing is added
nothing is taken away

One Afternoon

on the porch we sat in the afternoon
late summer like the fall
you two standing and me sitting
two young girls
and a too-rapidly aging father
quietly
no one saying a word

we knew it was special
sensing real magic
being together in silence
a rare moment
pure experience
you taught me a lesson

when I told your mother
she already knew
you told her because even you
had been startled

sometimes even poetry conceals
secrets too painful to tell
what your conscience whispers
but here I confess,
those moments were too few

Crime Scene

let us secure the border
the whole thing
with that yellow tape
you see on television

starting from the East Coast
down around to
the Gulf of Mexico
across the Mexican border
up the West Coast
across Canada
squaring the circle of shame

we need to gather evidence
take statements
expose the truth
that has been
conveniently forgotten

someone needs
to take responsibility
to be held accountable
there are questions
to be answered

who has been paid off?
what happened to our prosperity?
when will democracy return?

where are our freedoms?
how will our good name be restored?

therefore

we the people
of the United States
declare this nation
a crime scene
and demand justice
rather than pollutants,
avarice, rancor,
high hubris,
and low morals

Real Heroes

real heroes
may ride off
but they come home
by sunset
have rough hands
but tender hearts
can drive a hammer
or hold a child

give up a deer rifle
or a fishing trip
for braces
or a new bicycle
stay at jobs
that physically
and financially
break them
but pay the bills
that build a family

heroes fix old cars
in the cold
with used parts
building what they can
on weekends

and fix what they have to
at night

real heroes
keep promises
and commitments
raise children
rather than hell
say little
and do much
and do it
over and over

are underappreciated
and seldom understood
until it is too late
helping you
fulfill your dreams
at the cost of their own
they are
the plain men
of quiet character

when everybody else
leaves you
forgets you
real heroes
stand by you
believe in you

see something
others ignore
as long as they
draw a breath

and then maybe
a little longer
than that

My Mom

was born in a log cabin
nestled in a long valley
on a Missouri homestead
and still lives
less than five miles away

never finished high school
but finished everything else
like a family
which she loved
without question

never learned to drive
yet from scratch
can make a skirt or dress or quilts
can beans and beets and pickles
bake homemade apple pie and bread

survived breast cancer
two knee replacements
and me

Home From School

there is nothing so delicious
as a day home from school
just sick enough to stay home
not sick enough to feel bad

to lie abed
watch mysterious shows
you have never seen before
read what you want
eat Campbell's Chicken Noodle Soup
with Saltines
drink 7-Up to settle your stomach
look out the window in wonder
free from cares
experience a different rhythm
normally denied you

then there is that magical time
when your free day
overlaps with the routine
and you experience
a convergence of time
rare as a solar eclipse
it begins precisely
when the school bus stops
but you do not get off
because you're already home
you have been all day

Timothy Leary
and the School Bus

he was a beagle
named after the LSD
counterculture guru
a purebred
but no hunter
so Finas gave him to me
as a pet
and he deserves a poem

he had no bad habits
save one
and that was the chasing
of school buses
which he never caught
but one finally caught him

it happened
at the start of day
on that country road
that took me everywhere
back then
paved over now
that day it was still gravel
on which he lay there
still, broken, and bleeding

I fetched him back
loading him
in a red Radio Flyer
the only ambulance I had
he lying flat and still
I parked him in the shade
there in front of the house
before going to school
lacking courage

so I left him there
not strong enough to shoot him
the manly thing to do
I could not even touch the .22
that lay inside unused
I just left him
all day feeling guilty
knowing he would suffer
alone

when I got home
that dog was gone
that wagon was empty
just standing
where I had left it
then soundlessly
there he was
come up from the woods
where he had waited
for me

he lived five more years
never
chased a school bus again
that broke him
and taught me
to let God make
the life-and-death choices
and not to chase
school buses

Welcome

opening

small

the

is

birth

in

to

a

big

world

So Now What?

the old ones
believed in demons
chatted up angels
performed magic
dreamed dreams
believed in something
somewhere
the Other

hoped for redemption
if not now
then later
if not here
then there

now we believe in nothing
the magic is gone
demons are impolite
rarely mentioned
except in mad ravings

we worship
science and things
our new gods
inorganic, cold, and alien
now even that fails
as surely as Zeus or Baal
so we are left little
and quite alone

Rain on a Tin Roof

rain on a tin roof
is not gentle
but amplified
exaggerated and full
a cacophony
such that the uninitiated
imagine a downpour
with even
the most gentle shower
while the experienced
divine a drizzle
for what it is
a drizzle
that contains
a curiously
pleasant hypnotic
you welcome
as you learn
to discount
the multiplication
of intensity

too many
hear that rain
on the tin roof
and panic
thinking it is
the end of times

or the end of them
or maybe just
the end
of something comfortable

the experienced
adjust and calculate
according to
accumulated wisdom
tempered by experience
measuring their lives
more carefully

Pallbearer

slipping on ground-flush
markers of stone
we carried Elaine
through dervish snow

Woodcraft

here are lessons learned as a country child
a stick in hand when you walk in the woods
keeps balance so your footing is sure
and wave that toy sword in front of you
to cut the invisible spider threads
that lie across the forest trail in ambush
silken webs that stick to your face and itch

walk quietly without shuffling feet
walk carefully to avoid dry leaves
stop still sometimes to listen for others
who follow or whom you may chance upon
mark your trail with bent twigs
and landmarks such as rocks
stacked one on another

Special Education

tucked away in the basement
in the concrete building
at the end of the hall
by the back door
just down from the bathrooms
with one lone teacher
she was short with black hair
she was awfully young
as much an outcast as they
who did not fraternize
she never spoke either
as she escorted them down the hall
all in a row like imprinted ducklings
with occasional sidelong glances
as they waddled past
with the eyes of victims
stopping at the water cooler
they flocked self-consciously
not knowing where to put their hands
an anonymous gaggle
of socially constructed misfits
with the patina of factory seconds
blended ages
of all shapes and sizes
some tall and gangly
others quite diminutive
they never did Band
nor sports

nor showed up after hours
for anything
not even the Christmas pageant
even had recess by themselves
nesting
in one little patch of playground
we tried not to stare
but grew quiet when they passed by
like them, not knowing
where to look or what to say
where to put our hands
for sure, we never waved
we never said hi
we hardly spoke of them
among ourselves
even to make fun
they were the excluded
even from ridicule
the secluded
the educationally damned

Winter

Winter is nothing
but the full-term
pregnancy of spring

'57 Chevy

We left to pick up my mom, who was
working that Saturday, riding in my dad's
'57 Chevy before seat belts before '57
Chevys were kool or even collectors' items
just an old car working guys drove for
cheap I rode up front unbuckled, of course,
since in those days you just sort of bounced
and slid around for better or worse in that
car on a hot summer day with the windows
down the radio was playing in mono AM
which is all we had then as my father sang
there in that car just as we passed over the
Perche Creek bridge the one that is now a
ruin I looked up at him as if for the first
time and was awed he seemed so human so
alive so happy it was a magic moment I had
never seen my dad sing before except to
mumble along like everyone else in church
anonymously I believe we are still there
back then frozen in time forever as our
essence somehow lingers in the interior of
a ghost '57 Chevy suspended since some
moments are eternal with Dad still larger
than life me still little that song he sang
which I wish I could remember still in the
air I should ask him the name of the song
see if he remembers it this was all so long
ago though before my sister and brother

came along to muddle things up before it
all got too crowded and we sold the '57
Chevy for a Kingswood Estate station
wagon that had one seat that faced
backward

Logotherapy

at the end
of the day
what matters
is that
I am still here
no matter
how impoverished
or depleted
that I still care
about something
that I have
something to do
tomorrow
and beyond
however imperfect
however small
there is a source
of meaning
that shines
through
existential darkness
welcoming me
back

Waiting for Your Letter

you owed that letter
an excuse
an apology
a lie
something
anything
I would have read it over and over
in some corner place
where I could be alone
to decipher the plain
and hidden messages

yet the years were dumb
their silence rings in my ears at night
only to find voice in my dreams
during the dark hours
when memories ascend
from the abyss

it is not pleasant
sometimes I awake
believing the dream lies
for a moment
until reality descends
to mock and shame me
for false hope

there is no closure for me
no real end
only a demi life
of an unanswered why
that weighs me down
and anchors me in the past
requiring an effort
to swim against the tide
of abandonment and absence

I would
like to believe
that you struggle
maybe feel remorse
about what happened
own some regret
but that is not true
you never wrote that letter
not because you never cared
that would have been something
instead
you never thought to

Summer Rides

Stingray bikes
with banana seats and sissy bars
three-speed stick shifts
fat, drag slick rear tires

summer was heaven
riding mostly on gravel roads
dirt lanes and grassy trails
rarely on the blacktop

diverting to Nichols store
for a soda at 12 cents a bottle
outrunning dogs and lollygagging
we went home when we were hungry

Whispers of the Dead

every place you go
you leave your life scent
that remains there
absorbed
entombed
captured in place
a bit of your presence
your essence
left behind
with the memories
of what was
who was
and what can never be again

when you revisit those places
if you are still
you feel it though
and see it strangely
at the edges of reality
as if in
a dim faded mist
replaying
over
and over
again
those old times
those people
those loves and dreams

some fulfilled
others lost

the haunts remain
long after you leave
waiting
until you come back
tirelessly replaying
the tableau
of your drama
your story
from yesterday

when you return
you can ignore it
by becoming numb
or
be consumed
by opening up, but
regardless
those ghosts of you not yet dead
remain to haunt

and

when you do die
they remain still
hovering and
fading
but never completely disappearing
just receding

into part of the background
the ambiance
voices that whisper
to visitors
in the rustling wind
shadow plays
in the museum of your life
blending in
such that history
becomes stacked
overlaid in a montage
emitting the hum of life
barely audible
and indecipherable
except to ones
who dare listen

Sound

even silence has a sound
can roar mutely loud
move the bowels or the soul

Batman

as it turned out
he was a mistake
from St. Louis
but being a big city kid
that made him exotic
imported
so he must be better
a higher form of delinquent
he arrived
with some vague connection
to my cousin
that was ill-defined
and ill-omened

so we went to the woods
he, my cousin, and I
to this cave
we had found before
above the dry creek bank
with a smooth clay floor
split in the middle
where a trickle of water ran through
and this guy found a bat
I don't know where it came from

then he set that life on fire
wordlessly
with workmanlike focus
using lighter fluid

he carried with him
and a lighter

who carries lighter fluid?
the lighter we understood
for our Kools
but he came prepared
at another level
of evil

I have never witnessed
a more stupid, cruel, or useless act
to my credit I told him so
my cousin concurred
we lectured him
corrected him on the spot
unambiguously
as soon as we could find
our voices
being temporarily dumbstruck
at the horror

for the first time
I witnessed
an absence of a soul
a golem of sorts

the outing had gone bad
so we left

what happened
the rest of the day
I forget
but never
what happened in the cave
the boy never came back
and me and Michael Eugene
never spoke of that incident

and
we never went back
to that cave
he ruined it

how do you make a boy
who carries lighter fluid
as part of his kit
and ignites bats?
I didn't know

now I do
that boy was an apprentice
of sadism and despair
having learned it
in intimate symposiums
from dedicated teachers
a product of homeschooling

Awaiting Your Instructions

let me explain the dilemma I'm in
Christians say I have to believe
in Jesus

Muslims say
I must submit

I cannot make head
nor tail of Hindu dogma
and Buddhists
deny you exist
yet pray anyway

figure that out

they all have holy books
best read in the original
Greek, Arabic, Sanskrit, or Pali
convincing arguments
and beautiful sentiments
voiced through
preachers, printing presses,
web pages, social networks
want my time, money, and most of all
my soul

they say a person in the wilderness
may start in the right direction
but naturally walks in circles
when their way is lost
with a list to one side
that defines the curve

so, before me are the numbered days
with which I will occupy my time
strolling through your creation
awaiting your instructions
please advise when
I circle past now
or the next time

Trip to the Mall

the modern-day Beulah land
supplicants go
to sacrifice their earnings
past, present, and future

prophecy replaced
with popular culture
faces flushed from the heat
of the burning bush of marketing

taken by the spirit
speaking in tongues
healed by consumerism
communion in the food court

heeding the altar call
of fifty percent off
as the choir sings
a medley of pop muzak

Family Photos

they are so powerful
those old
grainy photos
taken with
cheap Instamatic
film cameras
with fixed focus
plastic lenses

I stare at them
and they lure me
back with familiar
haunting faces
home places
old times

I recognize my father
younger than me now
my grandparents
that uncle
he died too young
of diabetes

we are all
frozen in time
posed together
in those holiday photos
those Christmases
before it all fell apart

the resemblances abound
the likeness of one generation
is found in another

and there is me
the raw material
of who I am now
in the hard shadow
of emergent teen years
surrounded by
those who shaped
and created me
including younger cousins

at this moment
I want to
physically enter
the picture
that lost universe
which is represented
in that snapshot
physically crawl into
the stiff, curled
one-dimensional
photographic paper
to exist
with the departed
times, people, and places
represented there

just give me a half hour
fifteen minutes
to commune
I would settle for five minutes
or less

I would have
a lot to tell them
who should go to a doctor
what stocks to buy
but most of all
just hear them
touch them
just one more time
it would mean everything
but time defeats me

there is no one
with whom even to bargain
or plead that request
nobody has the key
to unlock that door
nothing can be done
to change that

I finally look away
with a feeling of loss
unrequited yearning
for something that was
but is no more
that was captured

once upon a time
on film

a blessing and a curse

but mostly
despite everything
I am glad to have
a pictorial epitaph
something
to remind me
even if painful
of them
those who are
still so vital
even in memoriam

those to whom
I am so inextricably
connected
far beyond
the mere snapshot
that helps me remember
like an abandoned
bookmark
in a novel
I read long ago
still faithfully
marking that one spot
so it will not be lost
something to hold onto

at least for now
before the pictures
fade forever

Cyborg Song

01000011011110010110001001101110
11100100110011100100000010100110l
1011110110111001100111

1. X = 0

2. #it was a dark
01101001011101000010000001101110
11000010111001100100000011000010 0
10000001100100011000010111001001l
01011

3. #no, wait
01101110011011110010110000100000 0
1110111011000010110100101110100

4. #in the beginning
01101001011011100010000001101000
11010000110010100100000011000100l
10010101100111011010010110111001l
0111001101001011011100110011l

5. #no
0110111001101111

6. #this has all been done
01110100011010000110100101110011 0
01000000110100001100001011100110 0
10000001100001011011000110110000l
00000011000100110010101100101011 0

11100010000001100100011011110110111101101
11001100101

7. #I need to proclaim in my tongue
010010010010000001101110011001010
110010101100100001000000111010001
101111001000000111000001110010011
011110110001101101100011000010110
100101101101001000000110100101101
110001000000110110101111001001000
000111010001101111011011100110011
10111010101100101

8. #the dialect of digital
011101000110100001100101001000000
110010001101001011000010110110001
100101011000110111010000100000011
011110110011000100000011001000110
100101100111011010100101110100011000
00101101100

9. #because
011000100110010101100011011000010
111010101110011011001010000110100
001010

10. #I am
01001001001000000110000101101101

11. X = X + 1

47

12. #the analog
01110100011010000110010100100000
11000010110111001100001011011000 1
10111101100111

13. #and
01110100011010000110010100100000
11000010110111001100001011011000 1
10111101100111

14. #the digital
01110100011010000110010100100000
11001000110100101100111011010010 1
1101000110000101101100

15. #the spawn
01110100011010000110010100100000
11100110111000001100001011101110 1
101110

16. #of
0110111101100110000011010000 1010

17. #mammon
01101101011000010110110101101101 0
1101111011011100000110100001010

18. #and
01110100011010000110010100100000
11000010110111001100001011011000 1
10111101100111

19. #machine
0110110101100001011000110110100001101001011011100110010100001101000001010

20. if X > 1 goto 22

21. if X = 1 goto 10

22. #fruitful
01100110011100100111010101101001011101000110011001110101101100

23. #and
01110100011010000110010100100000011000010110111001100001011011000101111011000111

24. #multiplied
01101101011101010110110001110100011010010111000001101100011010010110010101100100

25. #end
0110010101101110011001100100

I Did It

do I look
feel
sound
smell
different?

I am

yesterday in the wee hours
eyes blurred looking for truth
or just tawdry amusement
on the bumper-to-bumper information
highway

I filled out the form
became a minister
instantly

see for yourself

the records are safely locked
in the vaults of the Universal Life Church
Modesto, California
home of impulse ordination

Another Ginsberg Sighting

this poem will end
in disappointment
stick with it, though
because in the end
I will give you something
to make up for that
so you do not leave
empty-handed

I saw him today
Ginsberg
in the ice and snow
this early February
just two weeks before Valentine's Day
chipping the crystals off
his beloved Volkswagen bus

that bald pate
dark black hair
the bushy beard
both dyed out of vanity
what a card
we will forgive him his foibles
because they make him interesting
and approachably human

the Jewish Buddhist
or perhaps the Jewish Buddha
or at least an amoral bodhisattva
with Hare Krishna tendencies

what gave it away
was the whole Ginsberg package
the wry smile
how he talked
and gossiped
and grab-assed
with everybody
never knowing a stranger

he had the walk
that gaze of smart curiosity
the bard's twinkle
short and just
on the good side of dumpy
in a rumpled suit
and white shirt

he was not alone, though
driving was Neal Cassady
the beat-generation wheel man
hunkered down warm inside
smoking a cigarette and handsome
or at least it looked like Cassady

or perhaps I wanted it to be
just like I wanted it to be Ginsberg
as if all that dying
had never happened

but Wikipedia tells me
Ginsberg died at age 70
gives a date of April 5, 1997
the cause is
"liver cancer via complications of hepatitis"
look it up for yourself
it all looks pretty official

but that is not really true
or not really the whole truth
because here we are
you and me
having this discussion about Ginsberg
and how he even had Cassady with him
we can still run across people
who sort of look like them
and there is more

I have this big red anthology
collected poems from 1947–1980
a massive missive
right here in front of me
some surprisingly bad
some unbelievably good
just like any poet's work
and I have some recordings

so I can listen to him,
read him,
imagine him anytime I want
we all can

so maybe it was Ginsberg?
or maybe just enough of him
to say hello to in passing
because nothing
is ever really lost
including
the voice of every poet
the words of every poem
like any true art
it is all reabsorbed
we breathe it in and out continuously
we breathe him in and out continuously

now I have kept my promise
giving you something here at the end
reminding you
together we brought him back
together we bring him forward

Jesus Picture

in the free want ads last night
listed for sale:

" Jesus picture, $15."

then a telephone number
the same ad ran again tonight

so many questions

A Love Poem

we are not all witches
at least I think not
yet we all have familiars
that take the form of animals
or perhaps other things
like my twelve-year-old van
a white twelve-year-old
minivan
which is as married
and suburban
and middle class
as you can get
I love that van
which has taken us
to Florida
and to, of all places,
the Mall of America
schlepped the kids to camp
and back again
we have hauled
trash with it
talked trash in it
moved with it twice
and used it for theater seats
at the drive-in
I resisted at first
it has grown on me
has become a part of me

that I depend on
that has never failed us
though it has come close
like when the transmission went bad
now that van
is in the winter of its years
deemed too unreliable
for long trips
so it is semiretired
but I still wash it once a week
vacuum it out
familiar things
are a part of us
that we take for granted
and we mourn them
when they go
only then
providing them the honor
they did not receive
when they should have
so
tomorrow we will
take the white van
to visit my parents in it
while everything
is still working

Utility

we are tethered to
wires
pipes
lines
and radio waves
all of different lengths
that pulse, dance, and live
a separate life
vestiges of raw resources
energy
and information
transmuted
and metered out to us
pimped, pumped, and transmitted
woven
above
around
below
and through us
and these things
have a secret life
like demigods
with their own attendants
who serve them
as house slaves
while we heed
the demand for tribute
or face disconnection

Poems Not Written

for every poem I write
there is one not written
so there is no record
of some secret thoughts
doubts, loves, and desires
absurdities, hard truths, and lunacy

nothing left behind
to shock, shame, or startle
trust me, what you have read so far is mild

not every thought or desire
should be given voice
and some deserve
the eternal censor
of silence

Service at Eventide

at dusk
when colors run to gray
the red birds chirp
their office
presiding from their pulpits
of branches and leaves
regal Cardinals
in cathedrals of trees

Original Publishers

I gratefully acknowledge the editors and staff of these journals, which originally published the following poems. Thank you.

The Chaffey Review
    "Cowgirls"

The Houston Literary Review
    "Real Heroes"

Indigo Rising Magazine
    "Pallbearer"
    "So Now What?"

Kerouac's Dog Magazine
    "Another Ginsberg Sighting"

The Legendary
    "A Convertible at Night"

MediaVirus Magazine
    "Home From School"
    "Rain on a Tin Roof"
    "Timothy Leary and the School Bus"

Mouse Tales Press
    "Service at Eventide"

Shot Glass Journal
    "Trip to the Mall"

63

Spare Mule: Newsletter of the Missouri State
Poetry Society
"Utility"

SpoFest Spoken Word
"Home From School"
"The Party"

Thunderclap Press
"Batman"

The Toucan Magazine
"Welcome"

Vox Poetica
"My Mom"
"One Afternoon"

Word Salad Poetry Magazine
"I Did It"